THOUGHTS ON
THE EAST

THE NEW DIRECTIONS *Bibelots*

Thomas Merton

Thoughts on the East

With an Introduction
by George Woodcock

A New Directions

Bibelot

Publisher's Note: This book is dedicated to the memory of George Woodcock, who before his death wrote "Thomas Merton and the Monks of Asia," the general introduction, as well as the short preface to the last chapter, "On Varieties of Buddhism." The short paragraph following that preface, as well as the other chapter introductions were prepared in house. The material selected in *Thoughts on the East* has been taken from the following Thomas Merton works: passages for the chapter on Taoism, from *The Way of Chuang Tzu* (New Directions, 1965); for the chapter on Zen Buddhism, from *Mystics & Zen Masters* (Farrar, Straus & Giroux, 1976, by permission) and from *Zen & The Birds of Appetite* (New Directions, 1968); for the chapter on Hinduism as well as on the varieties of Buddhism, from *The Asian Journal of Thomas Merton* (New Directions, 1975); and for the chapter on Sufism, from *The Geography of Lograire* (New Directions, 1969).

Manufactured in the United States of America.
New Directions Books are printed on acid-free paper.
First published as a New Directions Bibelot in 1995.
Published simultaneously in Canada by Penguin Books Canada Limited

Library of Congress Cataloging-in-Publication Data
Merton, Thomas, 1915–1968.
Thoughts on the East / Thomas Merton ; with an introduction by George Woodcock.
p. cm.
"A New Directions bibelot."
ISBN 0–8112–1293–9
1. Christianity and other religions—Asian. 2. Asia—Religion. 3. Spiritual life—Comparative studies. 4. Mysticism—Comparative studies. 5. Monastic and religious life—Comparative studies. 6. Merton, Thomas, 1915–1968—Views on Asian religions. 7. East and West. I. Title.
BR128.A77M47   1995
291—dc20   95–5377
                                                                                                          CIP

FIFTH PRINTING

New Directions Books are published for James Laughlin
by New Directions Publishing Corporation,
80 Eighth Avenue, New York 10011

Contents

THOMAS MERTON AND
THE MONKS OF ASIA

THOMAS MERTON AND
THE MONKS OF ASIA

BY GEORGE WOODCOCK

As with many people whom we suspect of being geniuses,
Thomas Merton's breadth of vision lay largely in the self-
contradictory nature of his interests and urges, their apparent
fragmentation being a sign of a deep unity. He was a painstak-
ing priest of the Roman Church and a monk in one of the
strictest Catholic Orders, the Cistercians or Trappists. And
enclosed within the walls of the Abbey of Gethsemani in Ken-
tucky he remained, with few sallies into the outer world,
before that bold expedition to a monastic conference in Asia
that ended in his lonely and premature death. He was then a
man at the height of his literary and intellectual powers and of
his moral influence; perhaps the only man who could stand
beside him as a spiritual force was the Dalai Lama, with whom
he discoursed fervently and as an equal.

Even in Merton's early monastic life he showed the contrary
impulse, the urge away from the disciplines of congregational
activities. He began to experience the desire for the minimalist
and contemplative life of the hermit, and found that the Trappist rules were not so strict as he had imagined. In the great
wilderness area of Gethsemani he was allowed his cinder-block
hermitage, while he also took part in the collective activities of
the monastery. He was also encouraged to write and publish

1

under minimal censorship, and the monastery reaped his royalties. Merton started to write two kinds of verse: the poetry of the choir, poems of holy and collective celebration, full of triumphant noise and vivid, even gaudy imagery; and the very different poetry of the desert, austere and quiet, celebrating the unity of simplicity and true knowledge as projected years ago by the ancient hermits of the Egyptian desert.

From the beginning the poetry and the prose narratives Merton published established a surprisingly broad readership, not only among Catholics but also among dissenters of all kinds like the present writer. We were impressed by the lyrical talents of a young man who did not fit in with the general pattern of the poet in the 1940's and 1950's, but we were also intrigued, even as sceptics, by the revelations that Merton's prose works, like *The Seven Storey Mountain*, gave of the devout mind. Here was someone to whom one might listen, someone to arouse one's discursive urges. And Merton, by what is perhaps the decisive paradox of his existence, remained orthodox in doctrine even as he allied himself with the radical urges that were reshaping Catholicism. Vatican II's revision of the great Tridentine forms of the Counter-Revolution provided the authorization he needed to draw near to other men and women of eremitic inclinations and mystical aims. He opened his mind to the treasuries of Protestant (including Anglican) theology and experience. He tentatively began, almost from the beginning of his monastic career, to discover the great Asian religions like Buddhism and Taoism—many of them godless creeds in which the disciplines leading to insight were comparable to those of his fellow Catholic mystics.

In all of this Merton revealed yet another paradoxical aspect of his nature, or perhaps rather of his situation. Enclosed from the world as a Trappist monk, and seeking within the Order for ever greater degrees of eremitic solitude, he found himself encouraged by his superiors to publish his writings, which developed an extraordinary popularity for the works of a man not—in the literal sense—in the world of letters. And the interest in him carried on even after the great flood of converts and postulates into the church subsided.

Part of the reason for this was that Merton rarely wrote merely for churchmen and churchwomen. He used a kind of open eloquence that made his writings, even in their early more dogmatic stages, accessible to non-Catholics or even non-religious people, whether fellow poets or not. He had learnt the lesson of bringing the sinner to repentance, and it is significant that of all the great contemporary teachers he thought most highly of a thinker and a man of action who was only partly Christian. This was M. K. Gandhi, the Mahatma, who made the Hindu concepts of *ahimsa* and *satyagraha* a basis for his extraordinary campaigns of non-violent resistance that successfully dissolved the British Raj.

It was as late as 1965, less than four years before his death, that Merton began to publish the series of short books concerning his view of Asian religious beliefs as well as his own changes of perception. As a western, Christian monk, he embarked on an exploration of the great eastern traditions, Zen Buddhism and Lamaist Buddhism, Taoism, Hinduism and Sufism. *Gandhi on Non-Violence* appeared in 1965, and *The Asian Journal,* which came to an end with his sudden, tragic death in December 1968, was published in 1973.

In approaching them, however, we must not assume either that they represent a sudden shift in the attitudes of a strict Cistercian monk (as Merton had once attempted to be), or that they were in themselves finished and definitive works.

Long before he wrote specifically on the eastern teachers, he was reading—by the early 1940's—the writings of Aldous Huxley (such as *Ends and Means* and *The Perennial Philosophy*) concerning various mystical traditions. And certainly by the time he published *New Seeds of Contemplation* in 1961 he was in personal contact with the great Zen master, well known in the west, Daisetz Suzuki. (A good study relating Huxley and Merton remains to be written.)

Yet even to the end there was a touch of tentativeness, a kind of adumbrative caution about Merton's writing on the Asian thinkers and teachers. The Gandhi item is in fact a kind of handbook on Gandhi's sayings on the philosophy and practice of non-violence. Nowhere, when he writes of non-Christian religious communities, is there any evidence that he tried to know one of them by experience. His explorations tended to be through conversation and reading, and even then, especially in connection with Lamaist Buddhism, he did not always seem to talk to the right people. And here I suppose is the answer to the question that raises itself in one's mind. Why did he not take all this knowledge that lay in his mind and blend it into a major work on monasticism and mysticism? He was perfectly capable. Time and accident of course played their parts in preventing him, but there still seems a stubborn personal resistance to moving overtly into Ecumenism. Perhaps this is because in the world of mystic experience every man *is* his own church; there are no esoteric languages that can tell the ultimates of experience; and so in the end there is no real community of the spiritual. It is no matter of creed. It is a matter of each man's attitude to God or, in godless beliefs like Buddhism and Taoism, to the All.

This increase in interest in the great Asian beliefs during his last eight years coincided with great changes taking place in the world and even within the walls of Gethsemani. The old austere rule being relaxed, life in the monastery became more comfortable and less restricted. And in many ways the institution began to take on the character of a colander, still rigid in form but full of holes through which the influences of the outer world penetrated. One of these influences was a specifically American one. Thousands of young men, released from the army, flooded into the monasteries (and often out again almost as quickly) and, for a long period as Master of Novices and therefore spiritual director of these young men, Merton closely observed the minds of young Americans and was drawn into their concerns. The great movement for Black civil rights in the 1960's appealed to him as a militant Christian (he had earlier done social work in Harlem), and it was in writing about this that he first made himself heard as a social critic. He admired the methods of Martin Luther King, Jr. and his associates, and for the first time recognized the value and the validity of non-violent action. And thus it was through an American movement that he came to Gandhi, and through Gandhi and the *Bhavagad-Gita* to eastern philosphy in general. By this time he had become, for his books of poetry and on the contemplative life, something of an international celebrity, a man with whom such spiritual leaders as the Dalai Lama and the Zen philosopher Daisetz Suzuki would be pleased to discourse.

Merton's involvement with the Asian thinkers he chose to study and write about was usually limited. He was fascinated by Gandhi's argument that the *Bhagavad-Gita,* though on the surface an exhortation to war, is in fact a paean to the dedicated life, and he was intrigued that Gandhi had first found this Indian classic in an English translation in London while he was trying to become an imitation white man.

But Merton had little to say about Gandhi's advocacy of direct action. In his own way in fact he became an expert on the indirect and the oblique approach, and was much happier as an anthologist than as a profound interpreter. His introduction to Sufism consisted of a book or two and talking to an expert witness.

The Way of Chuang Tzu is perhaps the most interesting of these "Asian" books because it represents a good deal of reflection on Merton's part regarding a thinker who was perhaps as near as one could get to his own opposite. For Chuang Tzu, perhaps the greatest of all Tao teachers since the old original

Lao Tzu departed on the back of his blue buffalo, was a preacher of moral anarchy who quietly defied an emperor with his use of mockery.

Merton's closest and most intricate web of Asian contact was with the Tibetan Buddhists who had already been exiled for several years in India by the time of his visit there on the way to his monastical conference in Bangkok. The Dalai Lama had settled in his "palace" at Dharamsala, and a growing number of European and American students of Buddhism had made contact with him. Among them was Harold Talbott, a young American Catholic layman of ascetic temperament and some wealth, and I suspect Talbott helped to prepare Merton's way. The result, as it appears in *The Asian Journal*, was a curiously fragmentary view of Tibetan Buddhism.

To begin with, Merton became involved with a Sikkimese named Sonam Kazi, who acted as his guide to the Tibetan Buddhists. Described in *The Asian Journey* as a *great teacher*, in fact Sonam Kazi was a layman. Sonam Kazi had studied the religion not as a teacher in the Tibetan sense but as a devoté of one sect, the smallest if oldest of all the Tibetan groups, the Nyingmapa (Old Ones) and, except for the Dalai Lama, no teachers other than Nyingmapa appear in the narrative. It was rather like learning about Christianity from the Shakers, for while the Nyingmapa may be the oldest Tibetan sect, it is certainly less important historically than the other Red Hat sects (Kargyupa and Sakyapa), with whom Merton seems to have made no real contact. And—except for the Dalai Lama— he had no meetings with the Yellow Hat Geluppa Order, the Tibetan equivalent of the Church of England. Thus relatively minor teachers like Chatral Rimpoche (who ran a tiny gompa or monastery near Darjeeling) tend to be magnified in the narrative.

While Sonam Kazi urged Merton to follow extreme Nyingmapa meditational techniques, Chatral Rimpoche was suitably self-deprecating (thirty years of effort and no enlightenment). And the Dalai Lama was suitably cautionary, urging Merton to think twice before he adopted rigorous practices other than his own.

It may be worth noting here that while eastern meditation and contemplation in the Christian sense do overlap as quietistic religious practices, they are at root quite distinct. The main tenet of Mahayana Buddhism (*sunyata*) holds that all things are empty, or devoid of self-nature; the *Prajna,* the sixth and highest of their fundamental moral virtues of perfection (the Six *Paramita*), is a kind of insight into the truth of Emptiness. For Merton, however, contemplation is a state of fullness: "the religious contemplation of God . . . is a transcendent and religious gift." And as he stated in *New Seeds of Contemplation,* "It is not we who choose to awaken ourselves, but God Who chooses to awaken us." And so it is very unlikely that Thomas Merton, despite his curiosity and interest, ever meditated in the Buddhist sense.

Throughout their conversations the Dalai Lama shows that wonderful equality of intercourse which all who know him value. He does not set out to be your guru, and will not suggest a guru for you. He may warn of excessive enthusiasm, but in no way does he seek to command. One's sufficiency in one's space is what interests him, and so a conversation with him is always truly an exchange rather than a lecture. I am sure it was in this way, as a monk in the tradition of Sakyamuni (as he stresses), that he talked to Thomas Merton, a monk in the traditon of St. Benedict and the Desert Fathers.

Merton's death shortly after his encounter with the Tibetan Buddhists removes the ground for suppositions about the effect of these meetings. But I think we can say they must have deepened his devotion to the traditions of what Huxley called "The Perennial Philosophy": his Christian and above all his Trappist values would have been undiminished.

TAOISM

TAOISM

Lao Tzu (literally, The Old Philosopher) reputedly founded Taoism in China in the 6th century B.C. Preceding the arrival of Buddhism there by about 700 years, Taoism refers both to a system of thought and to a major Chinese religion. Taoism is mystical, devoted to transcending everyday life: its goal is to find the *Tao* (literally, the path), or the way of nature. Taoism's philosophical systems stem largely from the *Tao-te Ching* (*The Way of Virtue*), a text traditionally ascribed to Lao Tzu but probably compiled in the mid-3rd century B.C. Its parables and verses advocate intuitive and passive behavior in harmony with the cosmic unity underlying all things. The *Tao,* in the broadest sense, is the way the universe functions, characterized by spontaneous creativity or by regular alternations of phenomena (such as day followed by night) that proceed without effort. Effortless action can be seen in the conduct of water, which unresistingly accepts the lowest level yet wears away the hardest substance. Human beings, following the *Tao,* must abjure all struggle and learn the value of *wu-wei* (non-striving), through which one approaches a stage of creative possibility sometimes symbolized as a child or infant in Taoist writings. In a rough sense, what sin is to the Christian, cosmic disorder (or, at the local level, personal anxiety) is to the Taoist. The ideal state of being, fully attainable only by mystical contemplation, is simplicity and freedom from desire, comparable to that of "an uncarved block." Taoist laissez-faire political doctrines reflect this quietistic philosophy: the ruler's duty is to impose a minimum of government, while protecting his people from experiencing material want or strong passions. The social virtues expounded by Confucius were condemned as symptoms of excessive government and disregard of effortless action.

Second only to Lao Tzu as an exponent of philosophical Taoism was Chuang Tzu. "The humor, the sophistication, the literary genius, and philosophical insight of Chuang Tzu (c. 369–286 B.C.) are evident to anyone who samples his work," wrote Thomas Merton: "The collection of essays attributed to him, the *Chuang-tzu,* is distinguished by its brilliant and original style, with abundant use of paradox, satire, and seemingly nonsensical stories. But before one can begin to understand even a little of his subtlety, one must situate him in his cultural and historical context. That is to say one must see him against the background of the Confucianism which he did not hesitate to ridicule, along with all the other sedate and accepted schools of Chinese thought. . . . Chuang Tzu's chief complaint of Confucianism was that it did not go far enough. It produced well-behaved and virtuous officials, indeed cultured men. But it nevertheless limited and imprisoned them within fixed external norms and consequently made it impossible for them to act really freely and creatively in response to the ever new demands of unforeseen situations . . . ."

As time went by, Taoism changed somewhat, emphasizing the benefits flowing from the *Tao,* especially long life, and by the 5th century A.D., had become a fully developed religious system. With many features adopted from Mahayana Buddhism, offering emotional religious satisfaction to those who found Confucianism inadequate, Taoism developed a large deistic pantheon (probably incorporating many local gods), monastic orders, systems of magic, secret societies, and lay masters.

But in its early, formative period, when Chuang Tzu composed his essays, Taoism was a purely philosophic system, free of ecclesiastical organization. And at that stage, as Thomas Merton put it, "If there is a correct answer to the question: 'What is the *Tao?*' it is: 'I don't know.'" As Merton also once noted: "The whole secret of life lies in the discovery of this Tao which can never be discovered. . . .The world is a sacred vessel which must not be tampered with or grabbed after. To tamper with it is to spoil it, and to grasp it is to lose it."

The remarks prefacing Merton's five "imitations" from Chuang Tzu (which he describes as "free interpretative readings of characteristic passages that especially appealed" to him) are taken from his "A Study of Chuang Tzu," the foreword to *The Way of Chuang Tzu.*

THOMAS MERTON
ON TAOISM

The way of Tao is to begin with the simple good with which one is endowed by the very fact of existence. Instead of self-conscious cultivation of this good (which vanishes when we look at it and becomes intangible when we try to grasp it), we grow quietly in the humility of a simple, ordinary life, and this way is analogous (at least psychologically) to the Christian "life of faith." It is more a matter of *believing* the good than of seeing it as the fruit of one's effort.

The secret of the way proposed by Chuang Tzu is therefore not the accumulation of virtue and merit taught by Confucius but *wu wei,* the non-doing, or non-action, which is not intent upon results and is not concerned with consciously laid plans or deliberately organized endeavors: "My greatest happiness consists precisely in doing nothing whatever that is calculated to obtain happiness . . . Perfect joy is to be without joy . . . if you ask 'what ought to be done' and 'what ought not to be done' on earth to produce happiness, I answer that these questions do not have [a fixed and predetermined] answer" to suit every case. If one is in harmony with Tao—the cosmic Tao, "Great Tao"—the answer will make itself clear when the time comes to act, for then one will act not according to the human and self-conscious mode of deliberation, but according to the divine and spontaneous mode of wu wei, which is the mode of action of Tao itself, and is therefore the source of all good. . . .

The true character of wu wei is not mere inactivity but *perfect action*—because it is act without activity. In other words, it is action not carried out independently of Heaven and earth and in conflict with the dynamism of the whole, but in perfect harmony with the whole. It is not mere passivity, but it is action that seems both effortless and spontaneous because performed "rightly," in perfect accordance with our nature and with our place in the scheme of things. It is completely free because there is in it no force and no violence. It is not "conditioned" or "limited" by our own individual needs and desires, or even by our own theories and ideas. . . .

The key to Chuang Tzu's thought is the complementarity of opposites, and this can be seen only when one grasps the central "pivot" of Tao which passes squarely through both "Yes" and "No," "I" and "Not-I." Life is a continual development. All beings are in a state of flux. Chuang Tzu would have agreed with Herakleitos. What is impossible today may suddenly become possible tomorrow. What is good and pleasant today may, tomorrow, become evil and odious. What seems right from one point of view may, when seen from a different aspect, manifest itself as completely wrong.

What, then, should the wise man do? Should he simply remain indifferent and treat right and wrong, good and bad, as if they were all the same? Chuang Tzu would be the first to deny that they were the same. But in so doing, he would refuse to grasp one or the other and cling to it as to an absolute. When a limited and conditioned view of "good" is erected to the level of an absolute, it immediately becomes an evil, because it excludes certain complementary elements which are required if it is to be fully good. To cling to one partial view, one limited and conditioned opinion, and to treat this as the ultimate answer to all questions is simply to "obscure the Tao" and make oneself obdurate in error.

He who grasps the central pivot of Tao, is able to watch "Yes" and "No" pursue their alternating course around the circumference. He retains his perspective and clarity of judgment, so that he knows that "Yes" is "Yes" in the light of the "No" which stands over against it. He understands that happiness, when pushed to an extreme, becomes calamity. That beauty, when overdone, becomes ugliness. Clouds become rain and vapor ascends again to become clouds. To insist that the cloud should never turn to rain is to resist the dynamism of Tao. . . .

One of the most famous of all Chuang Tzu's "principles" is that called "three in the morning,"* from the story of monkeys whose keeper planned to give them three measures of chestnuts in the morning and four in the evening but when they complained, changed his plan and gave them four in the morning and three in the evening. What does this story mean? Simply that the monkeys were foolish and that the keeper cynically outsmarted them? Quite the contrary. The point is rather that the keeper had enough sense to recognize that the monkeys had irrational reasons of their own for wanting four measures of chestnuts in the morning, and did not stubbornly insist on his original arrangement. He was not totally indifferent, and yet he saw that an accidental difference did not affect the substance of his arrangement. Nor did he waste time demanding that the monkeys try to be "more reasonable" about it when monkeys are not expected to be reasonable in the first place. It is when we insist most firmly on everyone else being "reasonable" that we become ourselves, unreasonable. Chuang Tzu, firmly centered on Tao, could see these things in perspective. His teaching follows the principle of "three in the morning," and it is at home on two levels: that of the divine and invisible Tao that has no name, and that of ordinary, simple, everyday existence.

*See page 24.

15

Perfect Joy

Is there to be found on earth a fullness of joy, or is there no such thing? Is there some way to make life fully worth living, or is this impossible? If there is such a way, how do you go about finding it? What should you try to do? What should you seek to avoid? What should be the goal in which your activity comes to rest? What should you accept? What should you refuse to accept? What should you love? What should you hate?

What the world values is money, reputation, long life, achievement. What it counts as joy is health and comfort of body, good food, fine clothes, beautiful things to look at, pleasant music to listen to.

What it condemns is lack of money, a low social rank, a reputation for being no good, and an early death.

What it considers misfortune is bodily discomfort and labor, no chance to get your fill of good food, not having good clothes to wear, having no way to amuse or delight the eye, no pleasant music to listen to. If people find that they are deprived of these things, they go into a panic or fall into despair. They are so concerned for their life that their anxiety makes life unbearable, even when they have the things they think they want. Their very concern for enjoyment makes them unhappy.

The rich make life intolerable, driving themselves in order to get more and more money which they cannot really use. In so doing, they are alienated from themselves, and exhaust themselves in their own service as though they were slaves of others.

The ambitious run day and night in pursuit of honors, constantly in anguish about the success of their plans, dreading the miscalculation that may wreck everything. Thus they are alienated from themselves, exhausting their real life in service of the shadow created by their insatiable hope.

The birth of a man is the birth of his sorrow.

The longer he lives, the more stupid he becomes, because his anxiety to avoid unavoidable death becomes more and more acute. What bitterness! He lives for what is always out of reach! His thirst for survival in the future makes him incapable of living in the present.

What about the self-sacrificing officials and scholars? They are honored by the world because they are good, upright, self-sacrificing men.

Yet their good character does not preserve them from unhappiness, nor even from ruin, disgrace, and death.

I wonder, in that case, if their "goodness" is really so good after all! Is it perhaps a source of unhappiness?

Suppose you admit they are happy. But is it a happy thing to have a character and a career that lead to one's own eventual destruction? On the other hand, can you call them "unhappy" if, in sacrificing themselves, they save the lives and fortunes of others?

Take the case of the minister who conscientiously and uprightly opposes an unjust decision of his king! Some say, "Tell the truth, and if the King will not listen, let him do what he likes. You have no further obligation."

On the other hand, Tzu Shu continued to resist the unjust policy of his sovereign. He was consequently destroyed. But if he had not stood up for what he believed to be right, his name would not be held in honor.

So there is the question, Shall the course he took be called "good" if, at the same time, it was fatal to him?

I cannot tell if what the world considers "happiness" is happiness or not. All I know is that when I consider the way

17

they go about attaining it, I see them carried away headlong, grim and obsessed, in the general onrush of the human herd, unable to stop themselves or to change their direction. All the while they claim to be just on the point of attaining happiness.

For my part, I cannot accept their standards, whether of happiness or unhappiness. I ask myself if after all their concept of happiness has any meaning whatever.

My opinion is that you never find happiness until you stop looking for it. My greatest happiness consists precisely in doing nothing whatever that is calculated to obtain happiness: and this, in the minds of most people, is the worst possible course.

I will hold to the saying that: "Perfect joy is to be without joy. Perfect praise is to be without praise."

If you ask "what ought to be done" and "what ought not to be done" on earth in order to produce happiness, I answer that these questions do not have an answer. There is no way of determining such things.

Yet at the same time, if I cease striving for happiness, the "right" and the "wrong" at once become apparent all by themselves.

Contentment and well-being at once become possible the moment you cease to act with them in view, and if you practice non-doing (*wu wei*), you will have both happiness and well-being.

Here is how I sum it up:
Heaven does nothing: its non-doing is its serenity.
Earth does nothing: it non-doing is its rest.

From the union of these two non-doings
All actions proceed,
All things are made.
How vast, how invisible
This coming-to-be!

All things come from nowhere!
How vast, how invisible—
No way to explain it!
All beings in their perfection
Are born of non-doing.
Hence it is said:
"Heaven and earth do nothing
Yet there is nothing they do not do."

Where is the man who can attain
To this non-doing?

Confucius and the Madman

When Confucius was visiting the state of Chu,
Along came Kieh Yu
The madman of Chu
And sang outside the Master's door:
    "O Phoenix, Phoenix,
    Where's your virtue gone?
    It cannot reach the future
    Or bring the past again!
    When the world makes sense
    The wise have work to do.
    They can only hide
    When the world's askew.
    Today if you can stay alive
    Lucky are you:
    Try to survive!

    "Joy is feather light
    But who can carry it?
    Sorrow falls like a landslide
    Who can parry it?

    "Never, never
    Teach virtue more.
    You walk in danger,
    Beware! Beware!
    Even ferns can cut your feet—
    When I walk crazy

I walk right:
But am I a man
To imitate?"

The tree on the mountain height is its own enemy.
The grease that feeds the light devours itself.
The cinnamon tree is edible: so it is cut down!
The lacquer tree is profitable: they maim it.
Every man knows how useful it is to be useful.

No one seems to know
How useful it is to be useless.

Great Knowledge

Great knowledge sees all in one.
Small knowledge breaks down into the many.

When the body sleeps, the soul is enfolded in One.
When the body wakes, the openings begin to function.
They resound with every encounter
With all the varied business of life, the strivings of the
    heart;
Men are blocked, perplexed, lost in doubt.
Little fears eat away their peace of heart.
Great fears swallow them whole.
Arrows shot at a target: hit and miss, right and wrong.
That is what men call judgment, decision.
Their pronouncements are as final
As treaties between emperors.
O, they make their point!
Yet their arguments fall faster and feebler
Than dead leaves in autumn and winter.
Their talk flows out like piss,
Never to be recovered.
They stand at last, blocked, bound, and gagged,
Choked up like old drain pipes.
The mind fails. It shall not see light again.

Pleasure and rage
Sadness and joy
Hopes and regrets

Change and stability
Weakness and decision
Impatience and sloth:
All are sounds from the same flute,
All mushrooms from the same wet mould.
Day and night follow one another and come upon us
without our seeing how they sprout!

Enough! Enough!
Early and late we meet the "that"
From which "these" all grow!

If there were no "that"
There would be no "this."
If there were no "this"
There would be nothing for all these winds to play on.
So far can we go.
But how shall we understand
What brings it about?

One may well suppose the True Governor
To be behind it all. That such a Power works
I can believe. I cannot see his form.

Three in the Morning

When we wear out our minds, stubbornly clinging to one partial view of things, refusing to see a deeper agreement between this and its complementary opposite, we have what is called "three in the morning."

What is this "three in the morning?"

A monkey trainer went to his monkeys and told them: "As regards your chestnuts: you are going to have three measures in the morning and four in the afternoon."

At this they all became angry. So he said: "All right, in that case I will give you four in the morning and three in the afternoon." This time they were satisfied.

The two arrangements were the same in that the number of chestnuts did not change. But in one case the animals were displeased, and in the other they were satisfied. The keeper had been willing to change his personal arrangement in order to meet objective conditions. He lost nothing by it!

The truly wise man, considering both sides of the question without partiality, sees them both in the light of Tao.

This is called following two courses at once.

Where is Tao?

Master Tung Kwo asked Chuang:
"Show me where the Tao is found."
Chuang Tzu replied:
"There is nowhere it is not to be found."
The former insisted:
"Show me at least some definite place
Where Tao is found."
"It is in the ant," said Chuang.
"Is it in some lesser being?"
"It is in the weeds."
"Can you go further down the scale of things?"
"It is in this piece of tile."
"Further?"
"It is in this turd."
At this Tung Kwo had nothing more to say.
But Chuang continued: "None of your questions
Are to the point. They are like the questions
Of inspectors in the market,
Testing the weight of pigs
By prodding them in their thinnest parts.
Why look for Tao by going 'down the scale of being'
As if that which we call 'least'
Had less of Tao?
Tao is Great in all things,
Complete in all, Universal in all,
Whole in all. These three aspects

Are distinct, but the Reality is One.
Therefore come with me
To the palace of Nowhere
Where all the many things are One:
There at last we might speak
Of what has no limitation and no end.
Come with me to the land of Non-Doing:
What shall we there say—that Tao
Is simplicity, stillness,
Indifference, purity,
Harmony and ease? All these names leave me indifferent
For their distinctions have disappeared.
My will is aimless there.
If it is nowhere, how should I be aware of it?
If it goes and returns, I know not
Where it has been resting. If it wanders
Here then there, I know not where it will end.
The mind remains undetermined in the great Void.
Here the highest knowledge
Is unbounded. That which gives things
Their thusness cannot be delimited by things.
So when we speak of 'limits,' we remain confined
To limited things.
The limit of the unlimited is called 'fullness.'
The limitlessness of the limited is called 'emptiness.'
Tao is the source of both. But it is itself
Neither fullness nor emptiness.
Tao produces both renewal and decay,
But is neither renewal or decay.
It causes being and non-being
But is neither being nor non-being.
Tao assembles and it destroys,
But it is neither the Totality nor the Void."

ZEN

ZEN

Zen (in Chinese *Ch'an,* derived from the Sanskrit *dhyana* for meditation) is a Buddhist sect founded by the legendary Bodhidharma, who came to China from India in the late 5th century A.D. and taught the practice of "wall-gazing." Zen aims at the intuitive grasp of the truth of enlightenment as the direct seeing of one's "original mind" (which is Buddha), and places greater spiritual value on meditation than on scholarly knowledge, doctrine, ritual, particular scriptures, or the performance of good deeds. In its according pride of place to "sudden enlightenment" (*satori*), Zen was influenced both by Taoism and the important tenet of Mahayana Buddhism known as *sunyata* (Sanskrit for emptiness). The eight and ninth centuries were the "golden age" of Zen, which saw the development of a unique teaching style, stressing oral instruction and non-rational forms of dialogue (from which the *koan,* or paradoxical saying, was later derived). To jolt the student out of dependence on ordinary thought and into enlightenment, physical violence was sometimes used.

Two main Chinese schools of Zen, the Lin-chi and the Ts'ao-tung, were transmitted to Japan in the 14th century, where they flourished. The Rinzai (or Lin-chi) sect placed greater emphasis on the *koan* and effort to attain sudden enlightenment, while the Soto (or Ts'ao-tung) patriarch Dogen (1200–53) emphasized sitting in meditation (*zazen*) without expectation but with faith in one's intrinsic or original Buddha-nature. The austerity, discipline, and practical do-it-yourself nature of Zen made it the Buddhism of the samurai, and Zen monks occupied positions of political influence. Active in literary and artistic life, they also enormously influenced Japanese esthetics from poetry, painting and calligraphy to tea ceremonies and gardening. Japanese Zen went into decline in the 16th and 17th centuries, but its traditional forms were revived by the great master Hakuin (1686–1769). Zen meditation blossomed again, internationally, after World War II, and generated a vast amount of popular interest—and popular literature—by the time Thomas Merton wrote, warningly, in 1964, about the seriousness of Zen and its unsuitability for trendy dabblers:

"Where there is carrion lying, meat-eating birds circle and descend. Life and death are two. The living attack the dead, to their own profit. The dead lose nothing by it. They gain too, by being disposed of. Or they seem to, if you must think in terms of gain and loss. Do you then approach the study of Zen with the idea that there is something to be gained by it? This question is not intended as an implicit accusation. But it *is*, nevertheless, a serious question. Where there is a lot of fuss about 'spirituality,' 'enlightenment' or just 'turning on,' it is often because there are buzzards hovering around a corpse. This hovering, this circling, this descending, this celebration of victory, are not what is meant by the Study of Zen—even though they may be a highly useful exercise in other contexts. And they enrich the birds of appetite.

"Zen enriches no one. There is no body to be found. There birds may come and circle for a while in the place where it is thought to be. But they soon go elsewhere. When they are gone, the 'nothing,' the 'no-body' that was there, suddenly appears. That is Zen. It was there all the time but the scavengers missed it, because it was not their kind of prey."

THOMAS MERTON
ON ZEN

What, exactly, is Zen?

If we read the laconic and sometimes rather violent stories of the Zen masters, we find that this is a dangerously loaded question: dangerous above all because the Zen tradition absolutely refuses to tolerate any abstract or theoretical answer to it. In fact, it must be said at the outset that philosophically or dogmatically speaking, the question probably has no satisfactory answer. Zen simply does not lend itself to logical analysis. The word "Zen" comes from the Chinese *Ch'an,* which designates a certain type of meditation, yet Zen is not a "method of meditation" or a kind of spirituality. It is a "way" and an "experience," a "life," but the way is paradoxically "not a way." Zen is therefore not a religion, not a philosophy, not a system of thought, not a doctrine, not an ascesis.

• • •

Like all forms of Buddhism, Zen seeks an "enlightenment" which results from the resolution of all subject-object relationships and oppositions in a pure void. But to call this void a mere negation is to reestablish the oppositions which are resolved in it. This explains the peculiar insistence of the Zen masters on "neither affirming nor denying." Hence it is impossible to attain *satori* (enlightenment) merely by quietistic inaction or the suppression of thought. Yet at the same time "enlightenment" is not an experience or activity of a thinking and self-conscious subject. Still less is it a vision of Buddha, or an experience of an "I-Thou" relationship with a Supreme Being considered as object of knowledge and perception. However, Zen does not *deny* the existence of a Supreme Being either. It neither affirms nor denies, it simply *is*. One might say that Zen is the ontological *awareness of pure being beyond subject and object,* an immediate grasp of being in its "suchness" and "thusness."

But the peculiarity of this awareness is that it is not reflexive, not self-conscious, not philosophical, not theological. It is in some sense entirely beyond the scope of psychological observation and metaphysical reflection. For want of a better term, we may call it "purely spiritual."

In order to preserve this purely spiritual quality, the Zen masters staunchly refuse to rationalize or verbalize the Zen experience. They relentlessly destroy all figments of the mind or imagination that pretend to convey its meaning. They even go so far as to say: "If you meet the Buddha, kill him!" They refuse to answer speculative or metaphysical questions except with words which are utterly trivial and which are designed to dismiss the question itself as irrelevant.

When asked, "If all phenomena return to the One, where does the One return to?" the Zen master Joshu simply said: "When I lived in Seiju, I made a robe out of hemp and it weighed ten pounds."

This is a useful and salutary *mondo* (saying) for the Western reader to remember. It will guard him against the almost irresistible temptation to think of Zen in Neo-Platonic terms. Zen is *not* a system of pantheistic monism. It is not a system of any kind. It refuses to make any statements at all about the metaphysical structure of being and existence. Rather it points directly to being itself, without indulging in speculation.

● ● ●

The Zen insight, as Bodhidharma indicates, consists in a

direct grasp of "mind" or one's "original face." And this direct grasp implies rejection of all conceptual media or methods, so that one arrives at mind by "having no mind" (*wu h'sin*): in fact, by "being" mind instead of "having" it. Zen enlightenment is an insight into being in all its existential reality and actualization. It is a fully alert and superconscious *act* of being which transcends time and space. Such is the attainment of the "Buddha mind," or "Buddhahood."

· · ·

Zen insight is at once a liberation from the limitations of the individual ego, and a discovery of one's "original nature" and "true face" in "mind" which is no longer restricted to the empirical self but is in all and above all. Zen insight is not *our* awareness, but Being's awareness of itself in us. This is not a pantheistic submersion or a loss of self in "nature" or "the One." It is not a withdrawal into one's spiritual essence and a denial of matter and of the world. On the contrary, it is a recognition that the whole world is aware of itself in me, and that "I" am no longer my individual and limited self, still less a disembodied soul, but that my "identity" is to be sought not in that *separation* from all that is, but in oneness (indeed, "convergence"?) with all that is. This identity is not the denial of my own personal reality but its highest affirmation. It is a discovery of *genuine identity* in and with the One, and this is expressed in the paradox of Zen, from which the explicit concept of person in the highest sense is unfortunately absent, since here too the person tends to be equated with the individual.

· · ·

A Master saw a disciple who was very zealous in meditation.
The Master said: "Virtuous one, what is your aim in

practicing *Zazen* (meditation)?"
The disciple said: "My aim is to become a Buddha."

Then the Master picked up a tile and began to polish it on a stone in front of the hermitage.

The disciple said: "What is the Master doing?"
The Master said: "I am polishing this tile to make it a mirror."

The disciple said: "How can you make a mirror by polishing a tile?"
The Master replied: "How can you make a Buddha by practicing *Zazen!*"[10]

• • •

Another Zen master, Yuan-Wu, comments:

"Stop all your hankerings; let the mildew grow on your lips; make yourself like a perfect piece of immaculate silk; let your one thought be eternity; let yourself be like dead ashes, cold and lifeless; again let yourself be like an old censer in a deserted village shrine.

"Putting your simple faith in this, discipline yourself accordingly; let your body and your mind be turned into an inanimate object of nature like a piece of stone or wood; when a state of perfect motionlessness and unawareness is obtained, all the signs of life will depart and also every trace of limitation will vanish. Not a single idea will disturb your consciousness when lo! all of a sudden you will come to realize a light abounding in full gladness. It is like coming across a light in thick darkness; it is like receiving treasure in poverty. The four elements and the five aggregates are no more felt as burdens; so light, so easy, so free you are. Your very existence has been delivered from all limitations: you have become open, light and transparent. You gain an illuminating insight into the very nature of things, which now appear to you as so many

33

fairy-like flowers having no graspable realities. Here is manifested the unsophisticated self which is the original face of your being; here is shown bare the most beautiful landscape of your birthplace. There is but one straight passage open and unobstructed through and through. This is so when you surrender all—your body, your life, and all that belongs to your inmost self. This is where you gain peace, ease, nondoing and inexpressible delight. All the sutras and sastras are no more than communications of this fact; all the sages, ancient as well as modern, have exhausted their ingenuity and imagination to no other purpose than to point the way to this. It is like unlocking the door to a treasure; when the entrance is once gained, every object coming into your view is yours, every opportunity that presents itself as available for your use; for are they not, however multitudinous, all possessions obtainable within the original being of yourself? Every treasure there is but waiting your pleasure and utilization. This is what is meant by 'once gained, eternally gained, even to the end of time.' Yet really there is nothing gained; what you have gained is no gain, and yet there is truly something gained in this!"

• • •

Zen is consciousness unstructured by particular form or particular system, a trans-cultural, trans-religious, transformed consciousness. It is therefore in a sense "void." But it can shine through this or that system, religious or irreligious, just as light can shine through glass that is blue, or green, or red, or yellow. If Zen has any preference it is for glass that is plain, has no color, and is "just glass."

• • •

And in Zen enlightenment, the discovery of the "original face before you were born" is the discovery not that one *sees* Buddha but that one *is* Buddha and that Buddha is not what the images in the temple had led one to expect: for there is no longer any image, and consequently nothing to see, no one to see it, and a Void in which no image is even conceivable. "The true seeing," said Shen Hui, "is when there is no seeing."

What this means then is that Zen is outside all structures and forms. We may use certain externals of Zen Buddhist monasticism—along with the paintings of Zen artists, their poems, their brief and vivid sayings—to help us approach Zen.

The peculiar quality of Chinese and Japanese art that is influenced by Zen is that it is able to suggest what cannot be said, and, by using a bare minimum of form, to awaken us to the formless. Zen painting tells us just enough to alert us to what is *not* and is nevertheless, "right there." Zen calligraphy, by its peculiar suppleness, dynamism, abandon, contempt for "prettiness" and for formal "style," reveals to us something of the freedom which is not transcendent in some abstract and intellectual sense, but which employs a minimum of form without being attached to it, and is therefore free from it. The Zen consciousness is compared to a mirror. A modern Zen writer says:

> "The mirror is thoroughly egoless and mindless. If a flower comes it reflects a flower, if a bird comes it reflects a bird. It shows a beautiful object as beautiful, an ugly object as ugly. Everything is revealed as it is. There is no discriminating mind or self-consciousness on the part of the mirror. If something comes, the mirror reflects; if it disappears the mirror just lets it disappear . . . no traces of anything are left behind. Such non-attachment, the state of no mind, or the truly free working of a mirror is compared here to the pure and lucid wisdom of Buddha."
> (Zenkei Shibayma, *On Zazen Wasan,* Kyoto, 1967, p. 28)

What is meant here is that the Zen consciousness does not distinguish and categorize what it sees in terms of social and cultural standards. It does not try to fit things into artificially preconceived structures. It does not judge beauty and ugliness according to canons of taste—even though it may have its own taste. If it seems to judge and distinguish, it does so only enough to point beyond judgment to the pure void. It does not settle down in its judgment as final. It does not erect its judgment into a structure to be defended against all comers.

Here we can fruitfully reflect on the deep meaning of Jesus' saying: "Judge not, and you will not be judged." Beyond its moral implications, familiar to all, there is a Zen dimension to this word of the Gospel. Only when this Zen dimension is grasped will the moral bearing of it be fully clear!

• • •

As to the notion of the "Buddha mind"—it is not something esoteric to be laboriously acquired, something "not-there" which has to be there (where?) by the assiduous mental and physical pummeling of *Roshis, Koans* and all the rest. "The Buddha is your everyday mind."

The trouble is that as long as you are given to distinguishing, judging, categorizing and classifying—or even contemplating—you are superimposing something else on the pure mirror. You are filtering the light through a system as if convinced that this will improve the light.

• • •

The real way to study Zen is to penetrate the outer shell and taste the inner kernel which cannot be defined. Then one realizes in oneself the reality which is being talked about.

As Eckhart says:

> "The shell must be cracked apart if what is in it is to come out, for if you want the kernel you must break the shell. And therefore if you want to discover nature's nakedness you must destroy its symbols, and the farther you get in the nearer you come to its essence. When you come to the One that gathers all things up into itself, there you must stay." (Blakney, *Meister Eckhart,* p. 148)

A Zen *Mondo* sums it all up perfectly:

A Zen Master said to his disciple: "Go get my rhinoceros-
  horn fan."
Disciple: "Sorry, Master, it is broken."
Master: "Okay, then get me the rhinoceros."

• • •

We cannot begin to understand how the Zen experience is manifested and communicated between master and disciple unless we realize *what* is communicated. If we do not know *what* is supposed to be signified, the strange method of signification will leave us totally disconcerted and more in the dark than we were when we started. Now in Zen, what is communicated is not a message. It is not simply a "word," even though it might be the "word of the Lord." It is not a "what." It does not bring "news" which the receiver did not already have, about something the one informed did not yet know. What Zen communicates is an awareness that is potentially already there but is not conscious of itself. Zen is then not Kerygma but realization, not revelation but consciousness, not news from the Father who sends His Son into this world, but awareness of the ontological ground of our own being here and now, right in the midst of the world. We will see later that the supernatural Kerygma and the metaphysical intuition of the ground of being are far from being incompatible. One may be said to prepare the way for the other. They can well complement each other, and for this reason Zen is perfectly compatible with Christian belief and indeed with Christian mysticism (if we understand Zen in its pure state, as metaphysical intuition).

If this is true, then we must admit it is perfectly logical to admit, with the Zen Masters, that "Zen teaches nothing." One of the greatest of the Chinese Zen Masters, the Patriarch, Hui Neng (7th century A.D.), was asked a leading question by a disciple: "Who has inherited the spirit of the Fifth Patriarch?" (i.e., who is Patriarch now?)

Hui Neng replied: "One who understands Buddhism."

The monk pressed his point: "Have you then inherited it?"

Hui Neng said: "No."

"Why not?" asked the monk.

"Because I do not understand Buddhism."

This story is meant precisely to illustrate the fact that Hui Neng *had* inherited the role of Patriarch, or the charism of teaching the purest Zen. He was qualified to transmit the enlightenment of the Buddha himself to disciples. If he had laid claim to an authoritative teaching that made this enlightenment understandable to those who did not possess it, then he would have been teaching *something else,* that is to say a doctrine *about* enlightenment. He would be disseminating the message of his own understanding of Zen, and in that case he would not be awakening others to Zen in themselves, but imposing on them the imprint of his own understanding and teaching. Zen does not tolerate this kind of thing, since this would be incompatible with the true purpose of Zen: awakening a deep ontological awareness, a wisdom-intuition (*Prajna*) in the ground of the being of the one awakened. And in fact, the pure consciousness of *Prajna* would not be pure and immediate if it were a consciousness that one understands *Prajna*.

The language used by Zen is therefore in some sense an antilanguage, and the "logic" of Zen is a radical reversal of philosophical logic. The human dilemma of communication is that we cannot communicate ordinarily without words and signs, but even ordinary experience tends to be falsified by our habits of verbalization and rationalization. The convenient tools of language enable us to decide beforehand what we think things mean, and tempt us all too easily to see things only in a way that fits our logical preconceptions and our verbal formulas. Instead of seeing *things* and *facts* as they are we see them as reflections and verifications of the sentences we have previously made up in our minds. We quickly forget how to simply *see* things and substitute our words and our formulas for the things themselves, manipulating facts so that we see only what conveniently fits our prejudices. Zen uses language against itself to blast out these preconceptions and to destroy the specious "reality" in our minds so that we can *see directly*. Zen is saying, as Wittgenstein said, "Don't think: Look!"

Since the Zen intuition seeks to awaken a direct metaphysical consciousness beyond the empirical, reflecting, knowing, willing and talking ego, this awareness must be immediately present to itself and not mediated by either conceptual or reflexive or imaginative knowledge. And yet far from being mere negation, Zen is also entirely positive. Let us hear D. T. Suzuki on the subject:

> "Zen always aims at grasping the central fact of life, which can never be brought to the dissecting table of the intellect. To grasp the central fact of life, Zen is forced to propose a series of negations. Mere negation however is not the spirit of Zen . . ." (Hence, he says, the Zen Masters neither affirm nor negate, they simply act or speak in such a way that the action or speech itself is a plain fact bursting with Zen. . . .) Suzuki continues: "When the spirit of Zen is grasped in its purity, it will be seen what a real thing that (act—in this case a slap) is. For here is no negation, no affirmation, but a plain fact, a pure experience, the very foundation of our being and thought. All the quietness and emptiness one might desire in the midst of most active meditation lies therein. Do not be carried away by anything outward or conventional. Zen must be seized with bare hands, with no gloves on." (D. T. Suzuki, *Introduction to Zen Buddhism,* London, 1960, p. 51)

It is in this sense that "Zen teaches nothing; it merely enables us to wake up and become aware. It does not teach, it points." (Suzuki, *Introduction,* p. 38) The acts and gestures of a Zen Master are no more "statements" than is the ringing of an alarm clock.

All the words and actions of the Zen Masters and of their disciples are to be understood in this context. Usually the

Master is simply "producing facts" which the disciple either sees or does not see.

Many of the Zen stories, which are almost always incomprehensible in rational terms, are simply the ringing of an alarm clock, and the reaction of the sleeper. Usually the misguided sleeper makes a response which in effect turns off the alarm so that he can go back to sleep. Sometimes he jumps out of bed with a shout of astonishment that it is so late. Sometimes he just sleeps and does not hear the alarm at all!

In so far as the disciple takes the fact to be a sign of something else, he is misled by it. The Master may (by means of some other fact) try to make him aware of this. Often it is precisely at the point where the disciple realizes himself to be utterly misled that he also realizes everything else along with it: chiefly, of course, that there was nothing to realize in the first place except the fact. What *fact?* If you know the answer you are awake. You hear the alarm!

But we in the West, living in a tradition of stubborn egocentered practicality and geared entirely for the use and manipulation of everything, always pass from one thing to another, from cause to effect, from the first to the next and to the last and then back to the first. Everything always points to something else, and hence we never stop anywhere because we cannot: as soon as we pause, the escalator reaches the end of the ride and we have to get off and find another one. Nothing is allowed just to be and to mean itself: everything has to mysteriously signify something else. Zen is especially designed to frustrate the mind that thinks in such terms. The Zen "fact," whatever it may be, always lands across our road like a fallen tree beyond which we cannot pass.

Nor are such facts lacking in Christianity—the Cross for example. Just as the Buddha's "Fire Sermon" radically transforms the Buddhist's awareness of all that is around him, so the "word of the Cross" in very much the same way gives the Christian a radically new consciousness of the meaning of his life and of his relationship with other men and with the world around him.

In both cases, the "facts" are not merely impersonal and objective, but facts of personal experience. Both Buddhism and Christianity are alike in making use of ordinary everyday human existence as material for a radical transformation of consciousness. Since ordinary everyday human existence is full of confusion and suffering, then obviously one will make good use of both of these in order to transform one's awareness and one's understanding, and to go beyond both to attain "wisdom" in love. It would be a grave error to suppose that Buddhism and Christianity merely offer various *explanations* of suffering, or worse, justifications and mystifications built on this ineluctable fact. On the contrary both show that suffering remains inexplicable most of all for the man who attempts *to explain it in order to evade it,* or who thinks explanation itself is an escape. Suffering is not a "problem" as if it were something we could stand outside and control. Suffering, as both Christianity and Buddhism see, each in its own way, is part of our very ego-identity and empirical existence, and the only thing to do about it is to plunge right into the middle of contradiction and confusion in order to be transformed by what Zen calls the "Great Death" and Christianity calls "dying and rising with Christ."

Let us now return to the obscure and tantalizing "facts" in which Zen deals. In the relation between Zen Master and disciple, the most usually encountered "fact" is the disciple's frustration, his inability to get somewhere by the use of his own will and his own reasoning. Most sayings of the Zen Masters deal with this situation, and try to convey to the disciple that he has a fundamentally misleading experience of himself and of his capacities.

"When the cart stops," said Huai-Jang, the Master of Ma-Tsu, "do you whip the cart or whip the ox?" and he added, "If one sees the Tao from the standpoint of making and unmaking, or gathering and scattering, one does not really see the Tao."

If this remark about whipping the cart or the ox is obscure, perhaps another *mondo* (question and answer) will suggest the same fact in a different way.

A monk asks Pai-Chang, "Who is the Buddha?"
Pai-Chang answers: "Who are you?"

HINDUISM

HINDUISM

One of the world's oldest religions, Hinduism is practiced by the vast majority of the people of India. With dozens of sects and very little ecclesiastical organization, Hinduism, uniquely, claims no single historical founder. A synthesis of the religions of the Aryan invaders of India (c. 1500 B.C.) and the indigenous Dravidians, Hinduism has evolved over a 4,000-year period into a devotional and philosophical polytheism. The goal of believers (achieved, perhaps, over the course of many lifetimes) is union with Brahma, Infinite Being. Tolerant and inclusive, there are many variations of Hindu religious practice. As Nehru said, "Hinduism, as a faith, is vague, amorphous, many-sided, all things to all men. It is hardly possible to define it, or indeed to say definitely whether it is a religion or not, in the usual sense of the word. In its present form and even in the past, it embraces many beliefs and practices, from the highest to the lowest, often opposed to or contradicting each other. Its essential spirit seems to be to live and let live."

A social system as well as a religion, Hinduism depends as much on what a believer is and does—that is on, on birth rank and social conduct—as on any one belief. Hindu expressions of faith cut a wide swath from exacting intellectual taxonomies and high spiritual discipline to theatrical pageantry and lingam worship, but all paths to Brahma are respected, and include the worship of images enshrined in temples, the making of pilgrimages, belief in the efficacy of yoga and of asceticism, and great respect for a personal guru. The two most general

44

features of Hinduism are the caste system and acceptance of the Vedas, the most ancient sacred scriptures. The Upanishads, mystical and speculative works that expand and deepen the Vedas, state the doctrine that Brahma, the absolute reality that is the self of all things, is identical with the individual soul, or atman.

Hinduism in all its forms also accepts the doctrine of karma (or causality), according to which the individual reaps the results of his good and bad actions through a series of lifetimes. Also universally accepted is the goal of moksha (liberation from suffering and from the cycles of rebirth), which can be attained by eliminating the passions and through knowledge of reality and finally union with God.

The first phase of Hinduism was the religion of the priests (or Brahmins) who performed the Vedic sacrifice, by which proper relations with the gods and the cosmos were established. By about 500 B.C., Brahminism was challenged by non-Vedic systems, notably Buddhism and Jainism. The Brahmin elite responded by creating a synthesis that accepted yoga (an eight-stage discipline of self-control and meditation aimed at achieving "the cessation of the modifications of consciousness") and recognized the gods and image worship of popular devotional movements. Post-Vedic Puranas (a class of narrative poems which follow the *Mahabharata* and the *Ramayana,* the two greatest epics of India) also elaborate the myths of the popular gods. They describe the universe as undergoing an eternally repeated cycle of creation, preservation, and dissolution, represented by the trinity of Brahma the Creator, Vishnu the Preserver, and Shiva the Destroyer: all aspects of the Supreme. The fervent sects and groundswell of devotion produced poet-saints all over India who wrote religious songs and composed versions of the epics in their vernaculars, literature which plays an essential part in present-day Hinduism. There was also an increase of writings such as the Laws of Manu, dealing with dharma or duty, not only as applied to the

45

sacrifice but to every aspect of life, (Their basic principle is varna-ashrama-dharma—dharma or duty in accordance with varna or caste, and ashrama or stage of life.)

The present diversity of Hinduism can be seen in part as the survival of all the stages of its development side by side. The most popular deities include Vishnu and his incarnations Rama and Krishna; Shiva; and the elephant-headed god Ganesha; and the Mother-Goddess or Devi, who appears as the terrible Kali or Durga but also as Sarasvati, the goddess of music and learning, and as Laksmi, the goddess of wealth. All the gods and goddesses (of which there are reputedly 330 million) have numerous aspects, but all are regarded as different manifestations of the one Supreme Being.

The *Bhagavad-Gita* (The Song of the Blessed One), which interested Thomas Merton very much, is a philosophical dialogue between the god Krishna (The Blessed One) and the warrior Arjuna inserted in the *Mahabharata.* The supreme bhakti (or yoga of devotion) scripture of India and the best of all sources for knowledge of its ethical views, the *Bhagavad-Gita* teaches the karma yoga doctrine of action.

THOMAS MERTON ON
ON HINDUISM

The Significance of the *Bhagavad-Gita*

The word *gita* means "song." Just as in the Bible the *Song of Solomon* has traditionally been known as "The Song of Songs" because it was interpreted to symbolize the ultimate union of Israel with God (in terms of human married love), so the *Bhagavad-Gita* is, for Hinduism, the great and unsurpassed song that finds the secret of human life in the unquestioning surrender to and awareness of Krishna.

While the *Vedas* provide Hinduism with its basic ideas of cult and sacrifice and the *Upanishads* develop its metaphysic of contemplation, the *Bhagavad Gita* can be seen as the great treatise on the "Active Life." But it is really something more, for it tends to fuse worship, action, and contemplation in a fulfillment of daily duty which transcends all three by virtue of a higher consciousness: a consciousness of acting passively, of being an obedient instrument of a transcendent will. The *Vedas,* the *Upanishads,* and the *Gita* can be seen as the main literary supports of the great religious civilization of India, the oldest surviving culture in the world. The fact that the *Gita* remains utterly vital today can be judged by the way such great reformers as Mohandas Gandhi and Vinoba Bhave* both spontaneously based their lives and actions on it, and indeed commented on it in detail for their disciples. The present translation and commentary† is another manifestation of the living importance of the *Gita*. It brings to the West a salutary reminder that our highly activistic and one-sided culture is faced with a crisis that may end in self-destruction because it lacks the inner depth of an authentic metaphysical consciousness. Without such depth, our moral and political protestations are just so much verbiage. If, in the West, God can no longer be experienced as other than "dead," it is because of an inner split and self-alienation which have characterized the Western mind in its single-minded dedication to only half of life: that which is exterior, objective, and quantitative. The "death of God" and the consequent death of genuine moral sense, respect for life, for humanity, for value, has expressed the death of an inner subjective quality of life: a *quality* which in the traditional religions was experienced in terms of God-consciousness. Not concentration on an idea or concept of God, still less on an image of God, but a sense of *presence*, of an ultimate ground of reality and meaning, from which life and love could spontaneously flower.

It is important for the Western reader to situate the *Gita* in its right place. Whereas the *Upanishads* contemplate the unconditioned, formless Brahma, the Godhead beyond created existence and beyond personality, the *Gita* deals with brahman under the conditioned form and name of Krishna. There is no "I-Thou" relationship with the unconditioned Brahma, since there can be no conceivable subject-object division or interper-

*Vinoba Bhave (1895–1982), founder of the Bhoodan land reform movement. A saintly, Gandhi-like figure, Bhave walked through the Indian countryside, accompanied by his followers, attempting to persuade landowners to give part of their holdings to the peasants who have no land.

†This essay by Merton on aspects of Hindu philosophy was first published as the preface to *The Bhagavad Gita, As It Is,* with an introduction, translation, and authorized purport by Swami A. C. Bhaktivedanta (New York, Macmillan, 1968).

sonal division in him, at least according to Hindu thought. In Christianity, too, the Godhead is above and beyond all distinction of persons. The Flemish and Rhenish mystics described it as beyond all form, distinction, and division. Unconditioned Brahma, the Godhead, is not "what we see," it is "who sees." "Thou art that." Unconditioned brahman is pure Consciousness. Pure Act—but not activity. Conditioned brahman is the "Maker" and "Doer," or rather the "Player" and "Dancer," in the realm of created forms, of time, of history, of nature, of life.

Conditioned brahman, then, appears in the world of nature and time under personal forms (various incarnations for Hinduism, one incarnation only for Christianity). Realization of the Supreme "Player" whose "play" (*lila*) is manifested in the million-formed inexhaustible richness of beings and events is what gives us the key to the meaning of life. Once we live in awareness of the cosmic dance and move in time with the Dancer, our life attains its true dimension. It is at once more serious and less serious than the life of one who does not sense this inner cosmic dynamism. To live without this illuminated consciousness is to live as a beast of burden, carrying one's life with tragic seriousness as a huge, incomprehensible weight (see Camus' interpretation of the myth of Sisyphus). The weight of the burden is the seriousness with which one takes one's own individual and separate self. To live with the true consciousness of life centered in Another is to lose one's self-important seriousness and thus to live life as "play" in union with a Cosmic Player. It is He alone that one takes seriously. But to take Him seriously is to find joy and spontaneity in everything, for everything is gift and grace. In other words, to live selfishly is to bear life as an intolerable burden. To live selflessly is to live in joy, realizing by experience that life itself is love and gift. To be a lover and a giver is to be a channel through which the Supreme Giver manifests His love in the world.

But the *Gita* presents a problem to some who read it in the present context of violence and war which mark the crisis of the West. The *Gita* appears to accept and to justify war. Arjuna is exhorted to submit his will to Krishna by going to war against his enemies, who are also his own kin, because war is his duty as a prince and warrior. Here we are uneasily reminded of the fact that in Hinduism as well as in Judaism, Islam, and Christianity, there is a concept of a "holy war" which is "willed by God," and we are furthermore reminded of the fact that, historically, this concept has been secularized and inflated beyond measure. It has now "escalated" to the point where slaughter, violence, revolution, the annihilation of enemies, the extermination of entire populations and even genocide *have become a way of life.* There is hardly a nation on earth today that is not to some extent committed to a philosophy or to a mystique of violence. One day or other, whether on the left or on the right, whether in defense of a bloated establishment or of an impoverished guerrilla government in the jungle, whether in terms of a police state or in terms of a ghetto revolution, the human race is polarizing itself into camps armed with everything from Molotov cocktails to the most sophisticated technological instruments of death. At such a time, the doctrine that "war is the will of God" can be disastrous if it is not handled with extreme care. For *everyone* seems in practice to be thinking along some such lines with the exception of a few sensitive and well-meaning souls (mostly the kind of people who will read this book).

The *Gita* is not a justification of war, nor does it propound a war-making mystique. War is accepted in the context of a particular kind of ancient culture in which it could be, and was, subject to all kinds of limitations. (It is instructive to compare the severe religious limitations on war in the Christian Middle Ages with the subsequent development of war by nation states in modern times—backed of course by the religious establishment.) Arjuna has an instinctive repugnance for war, and that is the chief reason why war is chosen as the example of the most repellent kind of duty. The *Gita* is saying that even in what appears to be most "unspiritual" one can act with pure intentions and thus be guided by Krishna consciousness. This consciousness itself will impose the most strict limitations on one's use of violence because that use will not be directed by one's own selfish interests, still less by cruelty, sadism, and blood-lust.

The discoveries of Freud and others in modern times have, of course, alerted us to the fact that there are certain imperatives of culture and of conscience which appear pure on the surface and are in fact bestial in their roots. The greatest inhumanities have been perpetrated in the name of "humanity," "civilization," "progress," "freedom," "my country," and of course "God." This reminds us that in the cultivation of an inner spiritual consciousness there is a perpetual danger of self-deception, narcissism, self-righteous evasion of truth. In other words, the standard temptation of religious and spiritually minded people is to cultivate an inner sense of rightness or peace, and make this subjective feeling the final test of everything. As long as this feeling of rightness remains with them, they will do anything under the sun. But this inner feeling (as Auschwitz and the Eichmann case have shown) can coexist with the ultimate in human corruption.

The hazard of the spiritual quest is of course that its genuineness cannot be left to our own isolated subjective judgment alone. The fact that I am turned on doesn't prove anything whatever. (Nor does the fact that I am turned off.) We do not simply create our own lives on our own terms. Any attempt to do so is ultimately an affirmation of our individual self as ultimate and supreme. This is a self-idolatry which is diametrically opposed to Krishna consciousness or to any other authentic form of religious or metaphysical consciousness.

The *Gita* sees that the basic problem of man is his endemic refusal to live by a will other than his own. For in striving to live entirely by his own individual will, instead of becoming free, man is enslaved by forces even more exterior and more delusory than his own transient fancies. He projects himself out of the present into the future. He tries to make for himself a future that accords with his own fantasy, and thereby escape from a present reality which he does not fully accept. And yet, when he moves into the future he wanted to create for himself, it becomes a present that is once again repugnant to him. And yet this is what he had "made" for himself—it is his karma. In accepting the present in all its reality as something to be dealt with precisely as it is, man comes to grips at once with his karma and with a providential will which, ultimately, is *more his own* than what he currently experiences, on a superficial level, as "his own will." It is in surrendering a false and illusory liberty on the superficial level that man unites himself with the inner ground of reality and freedom in himself which is the will of God, of Krishna, of Providence, of Tao. These concepts do not all exactly coincide, but they have much in common. It is by remaining open to an infinite number of unexpected possibilities which transcend his own imagination and capacity to plan that man really fulfills his own need for freedom. The *Gita,* like the Gospels, teaches us to live in awareness of an inner truth that exceeds the grasp of our thought and cannot be subject to our own control. In following mere appetite for power we are slaves of appetite. In obedience to that truth we are at last free.

SUFISM

SUFISM

The basic objective of Sufism—an umbrella term for the ascetic and mystical movements within Islam—is to gain knowledge of and communion with God through contemplation and trancelike ecstasy. The theories connected with the genesis of Sufism are varied, including that it stems from the esoteric doctrine of the Prophet Mohammed—"Whosoever knoweth himself, knoweth his God," and from neo-Platonist influences. And while Sufism is said to have incorporated elements of Christian monasticism, gnosticism, and Indian mysticism, its origins are traced to forms of devotion and groups of penitents (*zuhhad*) in the formative period of Islam, which was founded in the 7th century A.D. The word "sufi" first appeared in the 8th century A.D., probably in connection with the coarse woolen clothing worn by many of the ascetics ("suf" in Arabic means "wool").

Two central Sufi concepts are *tawakkul,* the total reliance on God, and *dhikr,* the perpetual remembrance of God. Despite orthodox opposition, Sufism was originally not unreconciliable with standard Islam, but the scholastic and ecstatic paths did diverge further in the 9th century with the Sufi concept of *fana* (or, the dissolution into the divine), and the emergence of organized Sufi orders (from the 13th century onwards). Sufi orders, which assimilated aspects of native religious traiditions, played an enormous role in the expansion of Islam into Africa and Asia. But despite this major contribution and their significant part in developing Muslim civilization (especially its literature and calligraphic art), Sufis have often been a target for orthodox Islamic factions. (Literary Sufism was characterized by the prominence of Persian works as well as the development of Urdu and Turkish mystic poetic genres.) Many conservative Moslems disagree with popular Sufi practices, particularly saint worship, the visiting of tombs, and the incorporation of non-Islamic customs. Despite difficulties with reformist and modernist Moslem movements, Sufism continues to be a charismatic facet of Islam.

"I am tremendously impressed with the solidity and intellectual sureness of Sufism," Merton wrote in a 1961 letter to Abdul Aziz: "There is no question but that here is a living and convincing truth, a deep mystical experience of the mystery of God our Creator Who watches over us at every moment with infinite love and mercy. I am stirred to the depths of my heart by the intensity of Moslem piety toward His Names, and the reverence with which He is invoked as the 'Compassionate and Merciful.'" His correspondence with Aziz, a Pakistani scholar of mysticism and especially Sufism, and study of the books they exchanged, inspired Merton to give a series of lectures (now lost) on Sufism to the monks at Gethsemani. Merton professed to Aziz a "deep sympathy for Sufism. It is highly practical, realistic, profoundly religious and set in the right perspective of direct relationship with the All-Holy God. Our conduct is based on His relation of Himself, not on mere ethical systems and ideals."

Merton's interest in Sufism also led him to write "Readings from Ibn Abbad" (in *The Geography of Lograire*), which he described as "simply meditative and poetic notations made on texts of Ibn Abbad." Ibn Abbad, a Moslem born in Spain in 1332, went to study in Morocco; and then, looking for the deeper meaning of the Koran, he joined a community of Sufis at Salé, attained mystical illumination (at Tangier, 1363?), and returned to the Holy City of Fez to guide and instruct others. About 1380 he was appointed Imam and preacher at the main mosque of Fez and exercised a powerful spiritual influence until his death in 1390. "Ibn Abbad," Merton notes, "taught that it is in the night of desolation that the door to mystical union is secretly opened, though it remains tightly closed during the 'day' of understanding and light. . . . The purpose of these notes is to share something of an encounter with a rich and fervent religious personality of Islam, in whom the zeal of the Sufis is revealed, in an interesting way, against the cultural background of medieval Morocco. There is a mordant, realistic, and human quality in the life and doctrine of this contemplative."

THOMAS MERTON
ON SUFISM

Readings from Ibn Abbad

1: *Ibn Abbad Described by a Friend* (Ibn Qunfud)

Among those I met at Fez, let me mention the celebrated
    preacher
The Holy Man Abu Abdallah Mahammad ben Ibrahim ben
    Abbad ar Rundi
Whose father was an eloquent and distinguished preacher.
Abu Abdallah is a sage,
A recollected man in whom renunciation and great kindness
    are one . . .
He speaks admirably of *Tasawwuf.* *
His writings are worthy to be read to the brothers as they
    practice *Dikr.* †
He never returns the visits of the Sultan
But he assists at spiritual concerts (*sama*) on the night of
    Mawlid. ‡
I have never found him sitting with anyone in a social gather-
    ing.

---

* *Tasawwuf*—Sufism: the way of poverty and mystic enlightenment.

† *Dikr*—systematic method of prayer and concentration in which breathing techniques are united with rhythmic invocation of Allah.

‡ *Mawlid*—feast of the nativity of the Prophet Mohammed.

57

Whoever would see Abu Abdallah Mahammad must seek him
　　out in his own cell.
At times I begged his prayers. This only made him blush with
　　confusion.
Of all the pleasures of this world he permits himself none
Save only perfumes and incense
Which he uses lavishly:
Indeed, the Sultan tried to equal him in this
But failed.
And Abu Abdallah Mahammad has taught
That the Holy Prophet himself
Used incense copiously to prepare for his encounters with
an　　gels.
He takes care of his own household affairs
And has never taken a wife or a mistress
For above all things he prizes peace
And tranquillity of soul.
At home he wears patched garments
And, when he goes outdoors,
A white or a green mantle.

2: *The Burial Place of Ibn Abbad*

He was buried in a vacant property, for he was a stranger
And had not built himself a tomb in that city, or in any other.
After a few years the wall of the lot fell down
But later, the City Governor
Built the saint a small dome,
Confiding to his secretary the care
To take up the offerings left there
And send them to the saint's family.

Meanwhile the Guild of Shoemakers
Took him as patron. Each year
On the evening of his death in Ragab*

* *Ragab*—June.

58

They come in procession for a vigil there
With lights, readings and songs,
For in his lifetime
The saint was their friend.
He sat in their shops, conversed with them.
He prayed for the apprentices
To save them from piercing awls
And giant needles.
Often in the Mosque
He led the shoemakers in prayer.
Today, however, he is forgotten.

3: *Prayer and Sermon of Ibn Abbad*

O Mighty One:
Let me not constrain
Thy servants!

O men:
Your days are not without change and number.
Life passes more quickly than a train of camels.
Old age is the signal
To take the road.
It is death that is truth,
Not life, the impossible!
Why then do we turn away from truth?
The way is plain!

O men:
This life
Is only a blinking eye.

O men:
The last end of all our desire:
May He draw close to us
The Living, the Unchanging.
May He move toward us

His huge Majesty
(If it be possible to bear it!)
His Glory!

O men:
Burn away impure desire
In His Glory!

4: *Desolation*

For the servant of God
Consolation is the place of danger
Where he may be deluded
(Accepting only what he sees,
Experiences, or knows)
But desolation is his home:
For in desolation he is seized by God
And entirely taken over into God,
In darkness, in emptiness,
In loss, in death of self.
Then the self is only ashes. Not even ashes!

5: *To Belong to Allah*

To belong to Allah
Is to see in your own existence
And in all that pertains to it
Something that is neither yours
Nor from yourself,
Something you have on loan;
To see your being in His Being,
Your subsistence in His Subsistence,
Your strength in His Strength:
Thus you will recognize in yourself
His title to possession of you
As Lord,

And your own title as servant:
Which is Nothingness.

6: *Letter to a Sufi Who Has Abandoned Sufism to Study Law*

Well, my friend, you prefer jurisprudence to contemplation!
If you intend to spend your time collecting authorities and
    precedents
What advice do you want from me?
I can tell you this: each man, today,
Gets what he wants,
Except that no one has discovered a really perfect
Way to kill time.
Those who do not have to work for a living
Are engrossed in every kind of nonsense,
And those who must gain their livelihood
Are so absorbed in this that they
Have time for nothing else.
As to finding someone capable of spiritual life
Ready to do work that is clean of passion
And inordinate desire
Done only for love of Allah—
This is a way of life in which no one is interested
Except a few who have received the special
Mercy of Allah.
Are you aware of this? Are you sure of your condition?
Well then, go ahead with your books of Law,
It will make little difference whether you do this
Or something else equally trivial.
You will gain nothing by it, and perhaps lose nothing:
You will have found a way to kill time.
As you say: you prefer to spend your time doing things you are
    used to.
Drunkards and lechers would agree:
They follow the same principle.

61

7: *To a Novice*

Avoid three kinds of Master:
Those who esteem only themselves,
For their self-esteem is blindness;
Those who esteem only innovations,
For their opinions are aimless,
Without meaning;
Those who esteem only what is established;
Their minds
Are little cells of ice.

All these three
Darken your inner light
With complicated arguments
And hatred of Sufism.
He who finds Allah
Can lack nothing.
He who loses Allah
Can possess nothing.

He who seeks Allah will be made clean in tribulation,
His heart will be more pure,
His conscience more sensitive in tribulation
Than in prayer and fasting.
Prayer and fasting may perhaps
Be nothing but self-love, self-gratification,
The expression of hidden sin
Ruining the value of these works.
But tribulation
Strikes at the root!

8: *To a Novice*

Be a son of this instant:
It is a messenger of Allah

And the best of messengers
Is one who announces your indigence,
Your nothingness.
Be a son of this instant,
Thanking Allah
For a mouthful of ashes.

9: *To a Novice*

The fool is one
Who strives to procure at each instant
Some result
That Allah has not willed.

10: *Letter to One Who Has Abandoned The Way*

Our friend X brought me your letter —one letter—
informing me of your present state. One letter, not two or
three as you contend. And thank God for it, since if there had
been two or three I would have had to answer them all and I
have no taste for that.

Since you have left me, your conduct is an uninterrupted
betrayal of Allah, the Prophet, the Law and the Way of Sufism.
And yet Allah had ennobled you in the state of poverty, and
had bound you more tightly than others to religion and *Tasaw-wuf*, so that your admiration of the friends of God had become
your life's breath. Thus you were obligated to remain faithful
and preserve this vocation from all that might corrupt it!

Yet you did nothing of the kind. You have taken the exact
opposite path. You have made all reconciliation impossible.
And worse: you have cast off religion entirely to run after trifles
that even fools would despise, let alone men of reason.

And on top of all that you have betrayed me for an onion, for
a turd, rather, since an onion can have some use!

Yet in spite of all this, there is the will of Allah which I do not measure; there is the power of Allah to which no limit can be imposed; and if Allah wishes to give the lie to my doubts of your possible conversion, that is not hard for Him to do.

As for me, I can help only by prayer.

But what help is that, if you do not help me by a sincere return?

Varieties

of

Buddhism

VARIETIES OF BUDDHISM

by George Woodcock

When Sakyamani, the historical Buddha, died in approximately 483 B.C., he left a flourishing movement that, like its companion Jainism, had arisen out of the heretical ferment in the Ganges Valley during the sixth century B.C. There was a vigorous *sangha* (or monastic order) and the body of orally transmitted doctrine of compassion and sympathy which attracted king and commoner. One king converted to the doctrine was Ashoka, the emperor of India, who sent a mission to Ceylon in 245 B.C. From there the teachings spread until both Burma and Indochina were converted. The doctrine and the tradition were recorded in Ceylon in the late first century B.C.; they constituted the body of writings called The Three Baskets, or Tripitake, and they have remained fairly unchanged over the centuries forming what we call Theravada, the Doctrine of the Elders.

At times in the past it has also been called Hinayana or the Lesser Vehicle, in contrast to Mahayana, the Greater Vehicle, and Vajrayana or Diamond Vehicle. The main difference between the two larger currents lies in their attitude towards the attainment of Nirvana, the state of detachment from the world at the time of death. Therevada is essentially a teaching of individual salvation in which the good deeds and ascetic feats of the *arhat* (or holy man) achieve his release from the wheel of life, from the cycle of death and rebirth. Laymen rarely qualify;

they have to wait until they are reborn in the favorable stance of a monk.

Mahayana, the Greater Vehicle, began to develop in the first century A.D. in Gandhara, in the northwest of India. Here a succession of Greek kings (notably Menander) and later Kushana princes, like Kanishka, were patrons of Buddhism. Here Hellenistic ideas of the ruler as *soter* (or savior) took root, and the idea of the *arhat* seeking his own nirvana was replaced by that of the *bodhisattva,* the Buddha-to-be who sacrifices his own release from the wheel of life to work on for other suffering beings.

It was this Mahayana Buddhism that was taken from Gandhara through central Asia on the Silk Road and led to wide conversions in China, Japan, and Korea. A Chinese mystical school, much influenced by Taoism, developed under the name of Ch'an, becoming Zen in Japan, a creed followed by artists and samurai.

Tibet was converted (though with much resistance from the native followers of the old shamanistic Bon doctrines) by Mahayanist teachers in the seventh century A.D., notably Padma Sambhava. In Bengal, from which these teachers had come, Buddhism had already been permeated by Tantric doctrines developed among the Hindus which combined mysticism, magic, and recognition of the female spirit that was sometimes, it is said, commemorated in controlled orgies.

In Tibet, Buddhism became hardly distinguishable from the Tibetan state. For centuries lay kings alternated with powerful monks in ruling the country. Buddhism split into a number of sects, including the original Nyingmapa (or Old Ones); the Kargyupa, which was most powerful in eastern Tibet and in the little border states of Bhutan and Sikkim; and the Sakyapa, whose head in the twelfth to thirteenth centuries was the priest king of Tibet. These older sects of monks are known collectively as Red Hats.

But the sect which enjoyed the most spiritual as well as

temporal power in Tibet during recent centuries has been the deliberate reform movement which among other things changed sartorial arrangements and became the Yellow Hats. (The "Hats" are a kind of headgear distantly reminiscent of a Greek plumed helmet and are worn at certain ceremonials.) Founded by a monk named Tsong Khapa in the early fifteenth century, the Yellow Hats' leader, eventually called the Dalai Lama, was appointed by converted Mongol princes in that century as the spiritual and temporal ruler of Tibet.

Most Tibetan monks, following as they do a mystical and sometimes magical route, would claim to be devotees of the Vajrayana. But not all Tibetans became Buddhists. Even now, in northern Nepal as well as in Tibet, there are remnant communities who adhere to the ancient shamanistic doctrines and practices of Bon.

In fact, by the end of the twentieth century the differences between the Tibetan sects do not seem to be fundamental, so much as habitual. All of them, leaders and followers, are willing to accept the Dalai Lama as the personification of their wishes.

—George Woodcock

• • •

The material which follows, taken from *The Asian Journal,* has been arranged in three parts: Merton's encounters with monks and rimpoches of the Nyingmapa order, whom he met with his guide Sonam Kazi; his interviews with the Dalai Lama; and, finally, to end this volume, his description of his deep mystical experience at Polonnaruwa. This was certainly one of the greatest spiritual events of Thomas Merton's life: "I was suddenly, almost forcibly, jerked clean out of the habitual, half-tied vision of things, and an inner clearness, clarity, as if exploding from the rocks themselves, became evident and obvious. . . ." Here he found the realization that "all matter, all life, is charged with *dharmakaya*" (the Sanskrit term for the cosmical body of the Buddha, the essence of all being). In Tibetan terms, this experience would be termed *dzogchen* (literally, "great perfection") or the Great Way of All-inclusiveness. *"Dzogchen,"* as L. P. Lhalungpa described it in *The Asian Journal*, "may be defined as the simplest and most beneficial way to rediscover instantly for oneself the transcendental awareness that is within, whose all-inclusive qualities are either presently active or lying latent in all human beings, thus dissolving in the process all discriminations such as ignorance and awareness."

THOMAS MERTON ON VARIETIES OF BUDDHISM

Meetings with Nyingmapa Monks and Rimpoches

Sonam Kazi is a Sikkimese who went to Tibet to consult doctors about an illness, then rode all over Tibet and took to meditation, studying under various lamas, including a woman lama in Lhasa. His daughter is supposed to be a reincarnation of this woman. She entranced Aelred Graham by reading comic books while he argued with her father. There is a sweet photo of her in the Desjardins book.

Sonam Kazi is a lay Nyingmapa monk. He has had several good gurus and seems far advanced in meditation. He is of course full of information but also of insight. He thinks I ought to find a Tibetan guru and go in for Nyingmapa Tantrism initiation along the line of "direct realization and dzogchen (final resolution)." At least he asked me if I were willing to risk it and I said why not? The question is finding the right man. I am not exactly dizzy with the idea of looking for a magic master but I would certainly like to learn something by experience and it does seem that the Tibetan Buddhists are the only ones who, at present have a really large number of people who have attained to extraordinary heights in meditation and contemplation. This does not exclude Zen. But I do feel very much at home with the Tibetans, even though much that appears in books about them seems bizarre if not sinister.

• • •

What is the purpose of the mandala? Sonam Kazi said one meditates on the mandala in order to be in control of what goes on within one instead of "being controlled by it." In meditation on the mandala one is able to construct and dissolve the interior configurations at will. One meditates not to "learn" a presumed objective cosmological structure, or a religious doctrine, but to become the Buddha enthroned in one's own center.

• • •

I talked to Sonam Kazi about the "child mind," which is recovered *after* experience. Innocence—to experience—to innocence. Milarepa, angry, guilty of revenge, murder and black arts, was purified by his master Marpa, the translator, who several times made him build a house many stones high and then tear it down again. After which he was "no longer the slave of his own psyche but its lord." So too, a Desert Father came to freedom by weaving baskets and then, at the end of each year, burning all the baskets he had woven.*

• • •

Sonam Kazi is against the mixing of traditions, even Tibetan ones. Let the Kagyudpa keep to itself. He suggests that if I edit a book of Tibetan texts, let them all be *one* tradition. A fortiori, we should not try to set up a pseudocommunity of people from different traditions, Asian and Western. I agree with this. Brother David Steindl-Rast's idea perplexed me a little—as being first of all too academic. But I had wondered about some different approach: a mere dream. And

*Tucci, Giuseppe: *The Theory and Practice of the Mandala,* tr. by A. H. Broderick, London, Rider & Co., pp. 83–84.

certainly no good in my own life. Now, since seeing the books the other night in Canada House, I am curious about re-exploring the Romanesque artistic tradition and the 12th-century writers in Christian monasticism in relation to the Eastern traditions . . . i.e., in the light thrown on them by the East.

Sonam Kazi spoke of acting with no desire for gain, even spiritual—whether merit or attainment. A white butterfly appears in the sun, then vanishes again. Another passes in the distance. No gain for them—or for me.

Down in the valley a bird sings, a boy whistles. The white butterfly zigzags across the top left corner of the view.

. . .

Man as body—word—spirit. Three ways of handling anger, lust, etc. Hinayana . . . Mahayana . . . Tantric.

. . .

The disciple, blindfolded, is led to the east gate of the prepared mandala. Blindfolded, he casts a flower on the mandala. The flower will find his way for him into the palace. Follow your flower!

. . .

I must ask Sonam Kazi about dreams. Tucci placed under his pillow a blessed leaf given him by the Grand Lama of Sakya. He dreamed of mountains and glaciers. (See Tucci, *op. cit.*, page 92.) A yellow butterfly goes by just over the heads of the small purple flowers outside the windows. Firecrackers explode, perhaps in the yard of the school. Hammering in the village.

Sonam Kazi criticized the facility with which some monks say nirvana and samsara are one, without knowing what they are talking about. Also, though it is true that "there is no karma," this cannot be rightly understood by many, for in fact there is karma, but on another level. He also liked the idea of Trappist silence at meals, at work, everywhere. He said the name Trappist was interesting since in Tibetan "trapa" means "schoolman" or monk. He likes Krishnamurti.

• • •

Sonam Kazi condemned "world-evasion," which he thinks ruined Buddhism in India. He would be against an eremitism entirely cut off from all contact, at least for me. But in another context he admired the recluses who severed all contacts, seeing only a few people or perhaps none at all, reserving special contacts only for a restricted list. Harold asked whether others would respect this arrangement. Sonam Kazi thought they would. When a hermit goes on full retreat he places a mantra, an image, and a seal on the outside of his cell, and the mantra reads: "All gods, men, and demons keep out of this retreat."

Cocks crow in the valley. The tall illuminated grasses bend in the wind. One white butterfly hovers and settles. Another passes in a hurry. How glad I am not to be in any city.

• • •

Gandhiji's broken glasses . . . Johnson has stopped the bombing. Two magpies are fighting in a tree.

Are Tantrism, and meditation on the mandala, the evocations of minute visual detail like the Ignatian method in some respects? And as useless for me? A white butterfly goes by in the sun.

One difference is the sixth point above the mandala's five points. The mandala is constructed only to be dissolved. One must see clearly the five points—or there is no sixth, which also includes them all. No six without five. The six make "eternal life." Note that when the body is regarded as a mandala, the five chakras (sex, navel, heart, throat, head) are completed by the sixth "above the head."

For the dissolution of a mandala the dusts and colors are taken in ceremony with the solemn snoring of trumpets and thrown into a mountain stream.

· · ·

The highest of vows, Sonam Kazi said, is that in which there is no longer anything to be accomplished. Nothing is vowed. No one vows it. Tibetans sacrifice their own gods and destroy spirits. They also mock, solemnly and liturgically, the sacrifice itself—a spirit in butter, an image of a god to be burned in a straw temple.

· · ·

I had a fine visit with Chobgye Thicchen Rimpoche, a lama, mystic, and poet of the Sakyapa school, one of the best so far. Sonam says Chobgye Thicchen is very advanced in Tantrism and a great mystic. He even knows how to impart the technique of severing one's soul from the body. He taught this to another lama who was later captured by Communists. The lama, when he was being led off to prison camp, simply severed soul from body—pfft!—and that was the end of it. Liberation!

We talked first about samadhi, beginning with concentration on an object, then going beyond that to meditation without object and without concept. I asked a lot of questions about bodhicitta, Maitreya and karunā. Bodhicitta, Thicchen said, is the most fundamental of these three concepts, which all center on love and compassion. He spoke of three kinds of bodhicitta: 1) "kingly"—in which one seeks spiritual power to save oneself and then save others; 2) "that of boatman"—in which one ferries oneself together with others to salvation; 3) "that of shepherd"—in which one goes behind all the others and enters salvation last—and this is the most perfect.

Chobgye Thicchen quoted something from the founder of the Sakyapa school that went more or less like this:

If you are attached to worldly things you are not a religious man.

If you are attached to appearances you cannot meditate.

If you are attached to your own soul you cannot have bodhicitta.

If you are attached to doctrines you cannot reach the highest attainment.

• • •

We started out early on a cold morning, about 7:45, in our friend's jeep with Jimpa Rimpoche and a big picturesque Tibetan type as guide to find other rimpoches. Also, Fr. Sherburne and Harold Talbott. I was feeling the cold as we hurried up the road toward Ghoom. I've had a bad throat; it seems to be aggravated by the coal smoke that fills the air. We went looking first for Chatral Rimpoche at his hermitage above Ghoom. Two chortens, a small temple, some huts. In the temple there is a statue of Padma Sambhava which is decorated with Deki Lhalungpa's jewels. But I did not see it. Chatral Rimpoche was not there. We were told he was at an ani gompa, a nunnery, down the road, supervising the painting of a fresco in the oratory. So off we went toward Bagdogra and with some difficulty found the tiny nunnery—two or three cottages just down behind the parapet off the road—and there was Chatral, the greatest rimpoche I have met so far and a very impressive person.

Chatral looked like a vigorous old peasant in a Bhutanese jacket tied at the neck with thongs and a red woolen cap on his head. He had a week's growth of beard, bright eyes, a strong voice, and was very articulate, much more communicative than I expected. We had a fine talk and all through it Jimpa, the interpreter, laughed and said several times, "These are hermit questions . . . this is another hermit question." We started talking about dzogchen and Nyingmapa meditation and "direct realization" and soon saw that we agreed very well. We must have talked for two hours or more, covering all sorts of ground, mostly around about the idea of dzogchen, but also taking in some points of Christian doctrine compared with Buddhist: dharmakaya . . . the Risen Christ, suffering, compassion for all creatures, motives for "helping others,"— but all leading back to dzogchen, the ultimate emptiness, the unity of sunyata and karuna, going "beyond the dharmakaya" and "beyond God" to the ultimate perfect emptiness. He said he had meditated in solitude for thirty years or more and had not attained to perfect emptiness and I said I hadn't either.

The unspoken or half-spoken message of the talk was our complete understanding of each other as people who were somehow *on the edge* of great realization and knew it and were trying, somehow or other, to go out and get lost in it—and that it was a grace for us to meet one another. I wish I could see more of Chatral. He burst out and called me a rangjung Sangay (which apparently means a "natural Buddha") and said he had been named a Sangay dorje. He wrote "rangjung Sangay" for me in Tibetan and said that when I entered the "great king-dom" and "the palace" then America and all that was in it would seem like nothing. He told me, seriously, that perhaps he and I would attain to complete Buddhahood in our next lives, perhaps even in this life, and the parting note was a kind of compact that we would both do our best to make it in *this* life. I was profoundly moved, because he is so obviously a great man, the true practitioner of dzogchen, the best of the Nyingmapa lamas, marked by complete simplicity and free-dom. He was surprised at getting on so well with a Christian and at one point laughed and said, "There must be something wrong here!" If I were going to settle down with a Tibetan guru, I think Chatral would be the one I'd choose. But I don't know yet if that is what I'll be able to do—or whether I need to.

Interviews with the Dalai Lama

November 4 / Afternoon

I had my audience with the Dalai Lama this morning in his new quarters. It was a bright, sunny day—blue sky, the mountains absolutely clear. Tenzin Geshe sent a jeep down. We went up the long way round through the army post and past the old deserted Anglican Church of St. John in the Wilderness. Everything at McLeod Ganj is admirably situated, high over the valley, with snow-covered mountains behind, all pine trees, with apes in them, and a vast view over the plains to the south. Our passports were inspected by an Indian official at the gate of the Dalai Lama's place. There were several monks standing around—like monks standing around anywhere—perhaps waiting to go somewhere. A brief wait in a sitting room, all spanking new, a lively bright Tibetan carpet, bookshelves full of the *Kangyur* and *Tangyur* scriptures presented to the Dalai Lama by Suzuki.

The Dalai Lama is most impressive as a person. He is strong and alert, bigger than I expected (for some reason I thought he would be small). A very solid, energetic, generous, and warm person, very capably trying to handle enormous problems—none of which he mentioned directly. There was not a word of politics. The whole conversation was about religion and philosophy and especially ways of meditation. He said he was glad to see me, had heard a lot about me. I talked mostly of my own personal concerns, my interest in Tibetan mysticism. Some of what he replied was confidential and frank.

In general he advised me to get a good base in Madhyamika philosophy (Nagarjuna and other authentic *Indian* sources) and to consult qualified Tibetan scholars, uniting study and practice. Dzogchen was good, he said, provided one had a sufficient grounding in metaphysics—or anyway Madhyamika, which is beyond metaphysics. One gets the impression that he is very sensitive about partial and distorted Western views of Tibetan mysticism and especially about popular myths. He himself offered to give me another audience the day after tomorrow and said he had some questions he wanted to ask me.

The Dalai Lama is also sensitive about the views of other Buddhists concerning Tibetan Buddhism, especially some Theravada Buddhists who accuse Tibetan Buddhism of corruption by non-Buddhist elements.

The Dalai Lama told me that Sonam Kazi knew all about dzogchen and could help me, which of course he already has. It is important, the Dalai Lama said, not to misunderstand the simplicity of dzogchen, or to imagine it is "easy," or that one can evade the difficulties of the ascent by taking this "direct path."

• • •

In the afternoon I got a little reading done and then had quite a good meditation. Talking with the various rimpoches has certainly been helpful, and above all the Dalai Lama himself. I have great confidence in him as a really charismatic person. The Tibetans are all quite impressive and their solidity does a great deal to counteract the bizarre reports about some of their practices. It is all very good experience.

November 6 / Second audience with the Dalai Lama

We drove up earlier, at 8:30, a bright, clear morning. More people and more trucks on the road: army trucks roaring around the corners, ambling buffaloes, students on their way to school, and the Jubilee Bus Company's silver dragons. At the entry to the Dalai Lama's residence there were pilgrims, maybe sadhakas, with marigolds on their hats or in their hair.

Most of the audience was taken up with a discussion of epistemology, then of samadhi. In other words, "the mind." A lot of it, at first, was rather scholastic, starting with sunyata and the empirical existence of things known—the practical empirical existence of things grounded in sunyata—enhanced rather than lessened in a way. I tried to bring in something about sila, freedom, grace, gift, but Tenzin Geshe had some difficulty translating what I meant. Then we discussed various theories of knowledge, Tibetan and Western-Thomist. There is a controversy among Tibetans as to whether in order to know something one must know the *word for it* as well as apprehend the concept.

We got back to the question of meditation and samadhi. I said it was important for monks in the world to be living examples of the freedom and transformation of consciousness which meditation can give. The Dalai Lama then talked about samadhi in the sense of controlled concentration.

He demonstrated the sitting position for meditation which he said was essential. In the Tibetan meditation posture the right hand (discipline) is above the left (wisdom). In Zen it is the other way round. Then we got on to "concentrating on the mind." Other objects of concentration may be an object, an image, a name. But how does one concentrate on the mind itself? There is division: the I who concentrates . . . the mind as object of concentration . . . observing the concentration . . . all three one mind. He was very existential, I think, about the mind as "what is concentrated on."

It was a very lively conversation and I think we all enjoyed it. He certainly seemed to. I like the solidity of the Dalai Lama's ideas. He is a very consecutive thinker and moves from step to step. His ideas of the interior life are built on very solid foundations and on a real awareness of practical problems. He insists on detachment, on an "unworldly life," yet sees it as a way to complete understanding of, and participation in, the problems of life and the world. But renunciation and detachment must come first. Evidently he misses the full monastic life and wishes he had more time to meditate and study himself. At the end he invited us back again Friday to talk about Western monasticism. "And meanwhile think more about the mind," he said as we left.

November 8

My third interview with the Dalai Lama was in some ways the best. He asked a lot of questions about Western monastic life, particularly the vows, the rule of silence, the ascetic way, etc. But what concerned him most was:

1) Did the "vows" have any connection with a spiritual transmission or initiation?

2) Having made vows, did the monks continue to progress along a spiritual way, toward an eventual illumination, and what were the degrees of that progress? And supposing a monk died without having attained to perfect illumination? What ascetic methods were used to help purify the mind of passions?

He was interested in the "mystical life," rather than in external observance.

And some incidental questions: What were the motives for the monks not eating meat? Did they drink alcoholic beverages? Did they have movies? And so on.

I asked him about the question of Marxism and monasticism, which is to be the topic of my Bangkok lecture. He said that from a certain point of view it was impossible for monks and Communists to get along, but that perhaps it should not be entirely impossible *if* Marxism meant *only* the establishment of an equitable economic and social structure. Also there was perhaps some truth in Marx's critique of religion in view of the fact that religious leaders had so consistently been hand in glove with secular power. Still, on the other hand, militant atheism did in fact strive to suppress all forms of religion, good or bad.

Finally, we got into a rather technical discussion of mind, whether as consciousness, prajna or dhyana, and the relation of prajna to sunyata. In the abstract, prajna and sunyata can be considered from a dialectic viewpoint, but not when prajna is seen as realization. The greatest error is to become attached to sunyata as if it were an object, an "absolute truth."

It was a very warm and cordial discussion and at the end I felt we had become very good friends and were somehow quite close to one another. I feel a great respect and fondness for him as a person and believe, too, that there is a real spiritual bond between us. He remarked that I was a "Catholic geshe," which, Harold said, was the highest possible praise from a Gelugpa, like an honorary doctorate!

The Experience at Polonnaruwa

I visited Polonnaruwa on Monday. Today is Thursday. Heavy rain in Kandy, and on all the valleys and paddy land and jungle and teak and rubber as we go down to the eastern plains. ("We" is the bishop's driver and the vicar general of the Kandy diocese, a Ceylonese Sylvestrine with a Dutch name.) By Dambulla the rain has almost stopped. The nobility and formality of an ancient, moustachioed guide who presents himself under a bo tree. We start up the long sweep of black rock, the vicar general lagging behind, complaining that he dislikes "paganism," telling me I will get much better photos somewhere else, and saying they are all out to cheat me. ("They" being especially the bhikkhus.) Over to the east the black rock of Sigiriya stands up in the distant rain. We do not go there. What I want to see is Polonnaruwa. The high round rock of Dambulla is also quiet, sacred. The landscape is good: miles of scrub, distant "tanks" (artificial lakes dating back to the Middle Ages), distant mountains, abrupt, blue, heads hidden in rain clouds.

At the cave vihara of Dambulla, an undistinguished cloisterlike porch fronts the line of caves. The caves are dark. The dirt of the cave floors under bare feet is not quite damp, not quite dry. Dark. The old man has two small candles. He holds them up. I discover that I am right up against an enormous reclining Buddha, somewhere around the knee. Curious effect of big gold Buddha lying down in the dark. I glimpse a few frescoes but those in this first cave are not so exciting. Later, some good ones, but hard to see. The guide is not interested in the frescoes, which are good, only in the rank of Buddhas, which are not good. Lines of stone and sandalwood Buddhas sit and guard the frescoes. The Buddhas in the frescoes are lovely. Frescoes all over the walls and roof of the cave. Scenes. Histories. Myths. Monsters. "Cutting, cutting," says the guide, who consents to show a scene he regards as worthwhile: now sinners being chopped up in hell, now Tamils being chopped up in war. And suddenly I recognize an intent, gold-faced, mad-eyed, black-bearded Ceylonese king I had previously met on a post card. It is a wood sculpture, painted. Some nice primitive fish were swimming on the ceiling, following a line of water in the rock.

Polonnaruwa with its vast area under trees. Fences. Few people. No beggars. A dirt road. Lost. Then we find Gal Vihara and the other monastic complex stupas. Cells. Distant mountains, like Yucatan.

The path dips down to Gal Vihara: a wide, quiet, hollow, surrounded with trees. A low outcrop of rock, with a cave cut into it, and beside the cave a big seated Buddha on the left, a reclining Buddha on the right, and Ananda, I guess, standing by the head of the reclining Buddha. In the cave, another seated Buddha. The vicar general, shying away from "paganism," hangs back and sits under a tree reading the guidebook. I am able to approach the Buddhas barefoot and undisturbed, my feet in wet grass, wet sand. Then the silence of the extraordinary faces. The great smiles. Huge and yet subtle. Filled with every possibility, questioning nothing, knowing everything, rejecting nothing, the peace not of emotional resignation but of Madhyamika, of sunyata, that has seen through every question without trying to discredit anyone or anything—*without refutation*—without establishing some other argument. For the doctrinaire, the mind that needs well-established positions, such peace, such silence, can be frightening. I was knocked over with a rush of relief and thankfulness at the *obvious* clarity of the figures, the clarity and fluidity of

83

shape and line, the design of the monumental bodies composed into the rock shape and landscape, figure, rock and tree. And the sweep of bare rock sloping away on the other side of the hollow, where you can go back and see different aspects of the figures.

Looking at these figures I was suddenly, almost forcibly, jerked clean out of the habitual, half-tied vision of things, and an inner clearness, clarity, as if exploding from the rocks themselves, became evident and obvious. The queer *evidence* of the reclining figure, the smile, the sad smile of Ananda standing with arms folded (much more "imperative" than Da Vinci's Mona Lisa because completely simple and straightforward). The thing about all this is that there is no puzzle, no problem, and really no "mystery." All problems are resolved and everything is clear, simply because what matters is clear. The rock, all matter, all life, is charged with dharmakaya . . . everything is emptiness and everything is compassion. I don't know when in my life I have ever had such a sense of beauty and spiritual validity running together in one aesthetic illumination. Surely, with Mahabalipuram and Polonnaruwa my Asian pilgrimage has come clear and purified itself. I mean, I know and have seen what I was obscurely looking for. I don't know what else remains but I have now seen and have pierced through the surface and have got beyond the shadow and the disguise. This is Asia in its purity, not covered over with garbage, Asian or European or American, and it is clear, pure, complete. It says everything; it needs nothing. And because it needs nothing it can afford to be silent, unnoticed, undiscovered. It does not need to be discovered. It is we, Asians included, who need to discover it.

The whole thing is very much a Zen garden, a span of bareness and openness and evidence, and the great figures, motionless, yet with the lines in full movement, waves of vesture and bodily form, a beautiful and holy vision.